5 Top Secrets to Wedding Planning Success

Plus

The Ultimate Secret

Paula A Burns

ISBN:1495380882
ISBN-13: 978-1495380884

DEDICATION

I dedicate this book to every bride who is anticipating her big day.
Embrace the experience!

CONTENTS

Acknowledgments   i

Preface

1   How to set that wedding budget   Pg 2

2   Beware the 'Let me help you' Trap   Pg 7

3   Supplier Service & Reliability   Pg 12

4   Venue Restrictions & What You Should Know   Pg 18

5   The Fine Print on Contracts....*Yawn*   Pg 22

6   The Ultimate Secret   Pg 25

ACKNOWLEDGMENTS

First of all, I would like to thank my incredible network of family, friends and business colleagues who have been a constant encouragement to me throughout my career and the writing of this book.

A special thank you to my brother John T Burns, who created all the illustrations throughout the book including the cover.

I would like to thank all the wonderful couples that I have worked with over the years, to create their special day. I have been able to draw on all this experience in order to make this book a reality.

I also want to say a huge thank you to the amazing suppliers in my team, without whom PAB Events & The Wedding Clinic could not be possible.

PREFACE

So you've decided to throw the biggest celebration of your life. Congratulations and excitement are in huge supply and now you just can't wait to go shopping for that wedding dress!

My advice? Savour the feeling. So many things will happen between now and your big day. No matter how well organised you feel you are at the moment, there will be many voices, opinions, choices and a considerable amount of money spent, whatever your budget.

Weddings are magical experiences. They are designed to transport you to a world you have never been in before, make you feel things you have never felt before and on many occasions, make you act completely out of character; especially in the planning stage.

This hand book is designed to start you off on your journey with my five key tips that will help to keep you grounded. I have also included some real life experiences from brides who have already gone through the process (the names have been changed to protect the identity of the individuals). At the end of each tip, I have provided some space for you to record your findings and experiences. There is also space on the last few pages for you to write your own personal notes.

As an extra special bonus you will find my Ultimate Secret immediately after Secret No. 5.

Congratulations on your engagement and remember......enjoy the journey!

'How much?'

SECRET NO. 1
HOW TO SET THAT WEDDING BUDGET

Do you really need a wedding budget? After all, you're getting married. How many other opportunities will you get to push the boat out? Isn't it just a case of 'it costs as much as it costs'? Sadly this is the opinion of many couples. Even if they do think there is a need to set a budget, the process used is to find all the products and services they need, price them up and then make a rough estimate of how much it is all going to cost.

The problem with this method is that because your time and experience are restricted, there is no guarantee that the prices you have been quoted are the best ones and therefore the budget you arrive at could be inflated.

You will find many figures being mentioned by industry experts, some of which will make you feel extremely uncomfortable and quite frankly, could cause you to break into a nervous sweat! There are also others that will make you feel as if you are saving a fortune but the actual service turns out to be far from what was promised at the time of booking.

The budget should be your choice right from the very beginning of planning. It's the amount of money that you feel comfortable spending and that doesn't make you wince every time someone says it out loud. I have spoken to many brides at the outset and the majority of them stare at me blankly when I ask them about the budget. It's a case of not wanting to feel embarrassed by quoting too low a figure. Alternatively, others tend to quote a figure they have heard mentioned in the industry.

Let's consider Jenny's situation........

When Jenny got engaged, her first thoughts were that she would need to spend between £12,000 and £15,000 to create her perfect wedding day. But Jenny & her fiancé Tom knew that they could only afford to spend £7,000, so Jenny set about finding ways to source everything they needed at a knock down price.

The main outlay was their venue and catering. All the wedding venues were quoting prices way out of their budget. In fact most of them were quoting prices that took up all of the budget! So as far as Jenny was concerned there was only one thing for it. There were some local venues offering function rooms for weddings. Some of them were even offering to throw in catering too. Jenny and Tom weren't hugely impressed with any of them but they were convinced they had no choice. After deciding on the venue they least hated, they continued to make decisions based solely on cost. Jenny also kept telling herself that everything would turn out beautifully on the day. She decided to make a number of items such as invitations and favours and sourced some 'pretty silk flowers' from a local shop. The wedding cake was made by a relative and a good friend offered to take the photos.

Jenny's wedding day arrived. Rather than feeling like a princess, Jenny felt on edge. She was no longer sure that what she had visualised would look as fabulous in reality. There had been constant issues with the venue and she was uncertain whether the 'good friend' would turn up to take the photos as other family priorities had surfaced. In the end Jenny & Tom had spent nearly £9,000 overall but couldn't for the life of them think what all of that money had been used for. Their wedding day came and went. Jenny was exhausted.

There was absolutely nothing wrong with Jenny & Tom's budget of £7,000. They only had 60 guests in the day and 100 in the evening. Finding a hall or a function room which can act as a blank canvas is an excellent idea. But finding quality products and services is what will transform that blank canvas and turn wedding dreams into a reality. Of course, it is important to add personal touches as much as possible, but be sure that the do-it-yourself decisions are not solely based on the fact that you want to save money. You will be amazed how much money you can save by getting help from professionals who can assist in finding quality and unique products and services, all within your budget.

So are you ready to set your budget? Let me give you your starting point. Think about how much you *don't* want to spend then work your way backwards until you arrive at a figure that you feel happy with. There is no hard and fast rule about how much you must spend on a wedding, so no matter how ridiculously low you think it is, agree on a figure and stick to it!

Write down the budget that makes you feel uncomfortable

£…………………… (A)

Now write down the figure you would absolutely prefer to spend

£……………….………(B)

Make a list of all the things you definitely want (use a separate sheet if you have to)

....

....

....

....

....

....

....

....

....

………………………………………………………………………………………………………

Cost the above and compare it against your budget B (Remember the golden rule; seek professional advice if you are unsure of the best rates in the market place)

Make a list of the 'Nice to have' in order of importance; only add these things if you can afford it.

………………………………………………………………………………………………

………………………………………………………………………………………………

………………………………………………………………………………………………

………………………………………………………………………………………………

………………………………………………………………………………………………

………………………………………………………………………………………………

Don't be afraid to return to your budget regularly. Review it, update it and make it your best friend.

'Thank you.....I think!'

SECRET NO. 2
BEWARE THE 'LET ME HELP YOU' TRAP

This is very similar to when someone moves into their first house or apartment. It's a big financial commitment so family and friends are falling over themselves to help. 'I have a set of saucepans I don't use', I'm changing my sofa so you can have my old one', 'I've got a spare mattress in the garage, would you like it?' And so it goes on. Before you know it, you have a house full of things you don't like and quite frankly make your new pad look like a bit of a jumble sale!

Sadly, a similar thing happens when you announce you are getting married. Relatives and friends everywhere suddenly develop skills that will create a wedding fit for royalty. Wedding organisers, cake makers, florists; you name it. From every angle you will find someone who knows someone who will be able to save you lots of money.

Beware.

Don't get me wrong. Weddings are a wonderful family affair and it's important to get help where you can. But try not to lose sight of what you want. Don't feel pressured into accepting things for your wedding because you don't want to offend. If you have always wanted a fairy tale chocolate wedding cake, a traditional iced fruit cake made by a close family member is not going to fulfill your dreams. And if you have always dreamed of elaborate centre pieces that take your breath away, a few flowers in a ceramic vase are going to seem more like a nightmare than a dream.

You will feel a lot of pressure. You must understand that your family will be treating this as their day as well. After all this is a rare opportunity to proudly celebrate with long lost relatives and that means showing that no expense has been spared! But spending huge amounts of money does not a great wedding make. Neither are great weddings made by allowing everyone you know the opportunity to practise their wedding creation skills on your special day!

Chances are you know what you want or have a very good idea. Do some research and search the internet and magazines for ideas and inspiration. Make a note of your choices. Your notes will keep you focused so that when help is offered you can explain exactly what you are looking for. If the 'helper' is unable to provide this, politely decline the offer and explain that it is more important to you that they be there on the day to celebrate with you without the stress of providing something for the day. If they love and respect you, they won't be offended.

Deborah felt completely overwhelmed when she announced that she was getting married. Here's her story............

Deborah comes from a very large family. She was always aware that everyone would want 'a piece' of her day and the most important task she had was to manage everyone's expectations while still standing her ground. What made it even more difficult was that both sets of parents were contributing substantial amounts to the wedding costs. Therefore they felt it was their right to get involved in the decisions as much as possible.

The advice started flying around the moment Deborah and her fiancé announced their engagement. Things didn't improve as the months went on. Deborah felt a huge pressure to accept all the help and ideas that was being offered and slowly she could see her wedding slipping away from her. Immediate action was called for before it was too late.

Deborah and her fiancé called an emergency meeting with their parents. They gently explained that the picture being created for their wedding bore no resemblance to what they really wanted. They made sure they stressed how much they loved them and the rest of the family but really needed to have the main control of what happened on their wedding day. Deborah understood that there were still family members who wanted to be involved in arrangements, so her compromise was that she chose certain areas where they were given clear specifications of what she wanted and all parties agreed to discuss and review options before they were finalised. By keeping control of the areas that meant the most to her and being firm about being kept in the loop with the areas she was happy to delegate, Deborah slowly began to feel less overwhelmed and more supported.

So let's start the first steps on being clear about what you want. Make a list of your ideas in relation to the following key tasks. Use another sheet of paper if you need to. Once complete, make a decision about whether you need to call an emergency meeting with family and friends!

Wedding Dress…………………………………………………………………………....................

…………………………………………………………………………………………….....................

Venue …………………………………………………………………………....................

……………………………………………………………………………………..……………………

Wedding Décor………………………………………………………………………………

……………………………………………………………………………………..……………………

Catering…………………………………………………………………………..………………

……………………………………………………………………………..……………………………

Wedding Transport…………………………………………………………....……………

…………………………………………………………………………………..……………………

Wedding Cake………………………………………………………………..…………………

………………………………………………………………………………..……………………………

Flowers (bouquets button holes etc)…………………………………………….....

....

Wedding Favours...

....

Wedding stationery...

....

Photographer..

....

Wedding Entertainment...

....

Don't be afraid to use your imagination and include elements of your personality where ever you can. This is what will make your wedding celebration unique to you.

"What do you mean the car I booked
isn't available? I need
to be at the church in 20 mins!"

SECRET NO. 3
SUPPLIER SERVICE & RELIABILITY

Make no mistake. You **will** get caught up in the glitz and glamour of what I affectionately call The Wedding Circus.

There is no shortage of wedding suppliers. The market is absolutely saturated with products and services offering to create 'Your Dream Day'. And my advice to you is.......enjoy it! Half the fun of preparing for a wedding is trying out the things on offer.

However what you must be careful of is offers that sound too good to be true, terms and conditions, experience and reliability.

Every year a new wave of wedding suppliers emerges promising to make all your wedding dreams come true. The packages look stunning and the prices are being squeezed to grab the brides attention.

Be sure to find out as much as you can about a supplier in terms of reliability and experience. Many suppliers start their business after having their own wedding. They loved the experience so much they want to do it over and over again. This doesn't mean that they are experts. Find out how long a supplier has been in business and try to get recommendations from other weddings they have worked on. No matter how good the service or the price seem, the last thing you want to do is book someone for your wedding in 18 months' time and find that they have disappeared off the wedding market with your hard earned deposit!

Once you get as far as receiving the contract, look over the fine print. What does the service involve? Is it everything you will need on the day of your wedding? Will this option give you as little stress as possible? If something went wrong, what are your rights?

Carla had decided that chair covers would be a great decor addition for her wedding but once she started to add up the price per chair from a local supplier, things started to get a bit expensive. So Carla decided to take on the do-it-yourself option. Great idea in principal but this is what happened ....

The covers arrived a couple of days before her wedding. Carla had already arranged for two of her friends to help her fit the covers but one was unable to make it due to work commitments. It was the day before the wedding and there were 120 chairs to cover - Carla had ordered 125 'just in case.' At the last minute she managed to draft in the help of a cousin who had travelled down just for the wedding. They set to work. It soon became clear that there was another price to pay for choosing a random supplier from a search on the Internet. At least 30 of her chair covers had snags, holes or stains. Some of the organza sashes were frayed. Neither

Carla nor her helpers knew how to tie the sashes with a flat bow to finish off the overall look. The whole fitting process took a lot longer than they anticipated. Of course the company offered a small compensation for the frayed sashes after the wedding, but this was no consolation.

So what should you be looking out for when you are about to book a supplier? I have listed some key things that can sometimes get over-looked.

Venue

Evening end time...

Capacity..

Ease of access for all suppliers...

Cancellation process..

Photographer

Pre shoot session included?...

What albums are included in the price quoted...

....

Is the photographer's style modern or traditional? And most importantly what do you want?...

Cake

Is delivery and set up included in the price?...

....

Is there cake stand & cake knife at the venue? You may have to hire or

purchase these separately..

....

Wedding car

Do you really need two cars or can you get away with 1 car making two trips?

....

Does the hire price include decorative ribbons outside the car?

....

Wedding entertainment

How much space will your live entertainment need?

....

Flexibility of DJ song choices...

....

Wedding décor

Confirm delivery & set up is included in the price..

....

Dry hire restrictions/compensation ....

Range of choices available ....

....

Flowers

Delivery costs (church, venue & personal bouquets & button holes to home address) .

....

....

....

Doing this extra work will take time and you may be tempted to rush this in favour of more 'glamorous' tasks. But setting strong foundations is what will make all the difference when your wedding day arrives. This is why the best Wedding Planners thrive on getting everything right behind the scenes, so that their brides and their guests can glide through the day stress free.

*"They didn't tell me the price
didn't include decorations!"*

SECRET NO. 4
VENUE RESTRICTIONS AND WHAT YOU SHOULD KNOW

Surely there is no such thing as venue restrictions? Isn't it all about finding your dream location and watching every aspect of your fairy-tale come true?

Now I'm not being pedantic here. Of course everyone knows there will be a certain amount of restrictions at a venue. After all it's not your house;

you are only hiring it for a few hours or at best for a day! But mark my words. Your emotions will get carried away.

Most brides searching for the perfect venue do so through 'rose tinted glasses'. This is how it has always been. The photos will take your breath away and transport you into a fairy tale world where absolutely nothing can go wrong. And so it should be. This is why I always assess every venue very carefully to understand what their limitations are and most importantly how they will affect a brides' day.

There are many wonderful wedding venues available, most in idyllic locations. What the beautiful photographs do not tell you is whether you can party into the wee small hours, or if the venue has to be vacated by 11.30pm. It is very easy to convince yourself that an early finish to your evening won't be a problem when you are absolutely smitten with a venue. But try not to make decisions when you are too emotional. Most venues will pencil a date in for you and hold it for two weeks until you decide. This should give you plenty of time to discuss the pros and cons with your other half and family.

When I met Danielle she had her heart set on a venue that could accommodate a ceremony and the wedding breakfast. She and her fiancé had already spent some time visiting a number of venues and many of them were not living up to their expectations. Based on the area they had chosen and the amount of money they wanted to spend, they were beginning to think that they had to choose either a great ceremony venue OR a great reception venue. When I discussed with them their reasons for keeping everything at one venue, it soon became clear that it was all about logistics. How easy would it be for their guests get from one venue to another and even more importantly, which two venues would make the best match?

After speaking to me they identified their most important requirements for the day (regardless of venue). I was then able to help them identify two wonderful venues and iron out all the logistical issues that were causing them sleepless nights. We were able to plan transport and arrivals, spectacular options for photographs and an extremely functionable and beautiful layout plan.

The venue and the food are core ingredients of your wedding celebration so, whether you like it or not, you are going to have to spend some time doing your homework to make sure you are not hit by any nasty surprises on the day. Be sure to take the following things into consideration.

Venue capacity day & evening. Remember. The size of your band or live entertainment will affect how much space you will have available for your guests .

....

Access areas. How restricted is the venue? Can you access all areas?

....

....

How flexible are the menus? ....

What are the bar licencing times? ....

General bar prices. Are these reasonable for your guests?

....

....

Does the venue have round tables or are all the tables rectangular? Which do you prefer?

....

....

How far is the bar located from the function room?

....

Is there a policy against the use of confetti or extras like fireworks, candles etc?

....

....

What time will you be able to access to set up / bring personal items?

....

'Oh Dear, what have I missed!'

SECRET NO. 5
THE FINE PRINT ON CONTRACTS.....*YAWN*

And now for the really boring bit!

Ask anyone and a significant amount of them will tell you. Reading the fine print thoroughly and carefully is not something many of us do. Why? Because it's fine print of course!! How many of us have enough time to go through pages of paperwork to understand just what we are signing up to? Surely nothing can go wrong that is *that bad*? But what would you class as *that bad*?

Everyone's expectations are different. What is a slight hiccup for one is an absolute catastrophe for another.

Fine print is created to give the supplier a safety net. It's the place where people congregate when something goes wrong or an unusual request is made. Love it or loathe it, it will be your supplier's best friend. It is for this very reason it should be yours.

One of the biggest mistakes that brides make, is assuming that the venue can be set up the day before the wedding. Brides make this mistake at their peril. Popular venues at peak times will have a wedding scheduled every day. Even if your venue is available the day before, getting access may incur additional cost. This means that it is likely your wedding will to be set up on your actual wedding day. So if you are the type of bride that likes to be involved and check every detail before the wedding, you will need to check your contract and enquire about set up restrictions at an early stage. This will give you time to share information and build confidence with someone who will ensure that all your instructions are carried out.

Avoid making assumptions. Promotional wording is designed to grab your attention and immerse you in a world of assumptions. Great package prices can mean that even the simplest of things are not included. For instance a three course menu may not include coffee at the end of a meal, the sparkly dance floor shown in an image is unlikely to be included with the package price offered and most importantly, date restrictions will certainly play a part in price options quoted.

Now before you start breaking out into a cold sweat about all the documents you are going to have to read, let me try and put your mind at rest. My advice is that it is perfectly OK to scan the fine print, but in doing so there are certain things you must look out for. If you are clear on these things you can pretty much ride the storm whatever happens. So take a look at the fine print from each of your suppliers and do a separate list of the following for each one:

Confirm what you will get and compare it to what you are expecting

Cancellation clauses

Time constraints

Payment schedule and methods

What will incur additional cost

What is prohibited

What the supplier will not be held responsible for

Refund policy

Keep all your contract notes in a safe place. Then relax. There is no reason why you need to spend the rest of your planning time in a state of panic. In the unlikely event that you have to revisit your notes, you will have everything you need to make quick decisions.

6
THE ULTIMATE SECRET

The secret I am about to share is the cement that will keep you sane throughout the whole wedding planning process. It is often over looked in favour of the belief that everyone will want be involved in your fabulous wedding world all of the time. Sadly for you, as the bride to be, this is not the case.

Of course all your friends and family are excited for you and will be keen to be involved in whatever way they can. But their own busy lives and commitments will mean that they cannot be fully immersed in your amazing pool of wedding preparations 24/7. After the initial euphoria that the announcement of your engagement brings, the world will settle back into their own lives but continue to dip in and out of the preparations when they are able to.

So here is the Ultimate Secret. From the very start of your planning, identify someone who will be your Wedding Planning Rock. This could be a sister, a best friend or a wedding planner. Regardless of whom you choose it is important that you choose someone. If you are choosing a sister or a best friend you will need to explain the importance of this role (A good wedding planner will already be aware). The person you choose will need to support you emotionally and sometimes physically. There will be times when you will feel you are about to explode with all the information being thrown at you. You will need to weigh up costs against requirements. There will be suppliers to visit and options to try out.

You will notice that I haven't mentioned choosing your mum as your Wedding Planning Rock. There is a good reason for this. Mums are extremely emotionally involved with their daughters weddings. It goes without saying that they will want to (and will probably be) very much involved with your wedding arrangements. But it is likely that you will have ideas that are very different to what is expected at a traditional wedding. It is also likely you will want to put your own stamp on things based on current trends. This means you have to have a place where you can clear your head, talk about frustrations and quite frankly do a little dance with each other every time a plan comes together.

I have provided a space below for you to record the name of your Wedding Planning Rock. Don't worry if you have to change this person half way through the process. Ultimately, it's about standing in your dress on your wedding day, looking that person in the eye and saying those unspoken words 'We did it. Thank you for your support.'

Name of your Wedding Planning Rock

....

Notes

Notes

www.ingramcontent.com/pod-product-compliance
Lightning Source LLC
Chambersburg PA
CBHW050904290526
45792CB00002B/702